My Leadership Journal

Personal Reflections on Great Leadership

This Journal Belongs to:

_____
[Your Name]

Volume # _____

From (date) _____

To (date) _____

My Leadership Journal

This notebook is important to me!
If you have found it, this means that I've lost it!
I would very much appreciate your sending it back to me—
I will cover the costs.

Here is my contact info, and I will give you a mailing address:
  Email address: _____
  Phone: _____

Thank you!

Developed by LeaderDevelopment, Inc. to help you in your growth as a leader. For tips on how best to use this Leadership Journal, please refer to page 4.

For more information on LeaderDevelopment, Inc. and the resources it offers, please visit www.leaderdevelopmentinc.com, or call 803-748-1005.

Published by The Gordian Publishing House
PO Box 212175, Columbia SC 29221.

Special discounts on bulk quantities are available to corporations, professional associations, and other associations. For more information, call 803-748-1005 or email info@leaderdevelopmentinc.com for LeaderDevelopment Inc.

Copyright © 2012 by LeaderDevelopment Inc. All rights reserved. Printed in the United States of America. All quotes without attribution are quotations from Antony Bell or LeaderDevelopment Inc. No part of this book may be used or reproduced without written permission except in the case of brief quotations embodied in critical articles and reviews. LeaderDevelopment Inc. and its logo are registered trademarks of LeaderDevelopment Inc.
Cover design: Jessica Coate.

Library of Congress Cataloging-in-Publication Data
LeaderDevelopment Inc.
My Leadership Journal
By LeaderDevelopment Inc.

ISBN: 978-0-9779182-1-8
First Edition First Printing 2012.

My Leadership Journal

Congratulations! You are holding in your hand a vital tool for your development as a leader. This notebook is a place for you to capture your thinking on leadership—whether from a book you're reading, a conversation you've just had, a movie you've just seen, or an article you've just read—whatever the source, this is a place for you to record your thoughts and observations about leadership.

Great leaders are writers. Leaders are readers, too, but great leaders are also writers. They don't write to be published (though some are); they write because they know that writing is important for at least two reasons. The first is simply to *remember*. For most of us, if we don't write it down, we are likely to forget.

The second reason is less obvious, but even more powerful: we write to help us *think*. Whether with a pen in our hands or a keyboard at our fingertips, writing is not primarily a physical exercise: it is a *mental* exercise. Writing forces us to think clearly; it's not until we commit a thought to paper that it takes on real substance and moves from woolly nebulousness to thoughtful precision. We write to know what we think. No wonder a pen has been called a mental crowbar!

It actually does much more: writing not only forces precision in our thinking, it actually *generates* thinking. The very act of writing produces ideas that would not exist without the act of writing. Writing is the midwife of creative thought. There's something that happens between the brain and the hand on the paper (or the fingertips on the keyboard) that unleashes this creative energy.

And here is the good news, especially if you did everything you could to avoid any college course that had the slightest whiff of writing: as a thinking tool, you don't have to write well! Your personal reflections are for your own private consumption, and for this, you don't have to be concerned about spelling, grammar, punctuation, or style.

So get ready for some great insights into great leadership . . . insights that *you* will generate. And you will find that this Leadership Journal will become a log book for your journey, a fascinating and indispensable record of your progress in your quest for great leadership.

Tips for Getting the Most Out of Your Leadership Journal

The more you use this tool, the more you will appreciate its value in helping you grow as a leader. Here are some tips to help you get the most out of it:

- Don't feel you have to write in it every day. This is not that kind of journal. The purpose of this journal is to record the thoughts, ideas, comments, questions, experiences, and quotes that you want to remember. In practice, there will be times when you have much to write, and others when you will have little.

- Don't worry about spelling, grammar, punctuation, or style. These reflections are for your own private consumption, and no one is going to see them unless you choose to show them to someone. If you don't write much, or if you have little confidence in your ability to write, this should be good news!

- Use the page with the lines, the right-hand side, to record your main thoughts. Use the blank page on the left to jot down a brief title for the entry (for example, if you are recording some thoughts on motivation from a conversation with a colleague, your title might be "Motivation—discussion with John"). You can also use the same page (the left-hand page) to come back later with additional thoughts on the same topic—to add to it, to refute it, to change it, or to affirm it. Much of the time, you won't want to come back, but sometimes you will.

- As you look at the blank page with its empty lines, don't be intimidated. Just start writing. Don't fall into the trap of thinking that your ideas have to be well-formulated before they even get to the page. In reality, the very act of writing will help you formulate your thinking. Writing clarifies thinking: it's writing that leads you to a well-formulated conclusion, not a well-formulated conclusion that leads to writing. Don't lose sight of the fact that this is a thinking tool, and as a thinking tool, writing well is secondary. You're not entering an essay contest; you're entering a thinking process.

- Keep your journal with you. When you travel or when you are working outside the office, take it with you. You never know when you'll want to jot something down. We've designed it so that it's easy to pack and carry.

- If you are stuck for what to write about, here are some questions to get you going:
    - What do I want to accomplish in my current role?
    - Who are the leaders around me whose leadership I respect and want to emulate?
    - What examples of bad leadership do I observe? How can I avoid those pitfalls myself?
    - What is critical to the success of my team and the unit I am leading?
    - What is really important to me that I want to see in the behaviors of those I lead? What are the values I want to see characterize our team and our unit?
    - What recent experiences reflect my strengths?
    - What recent experiences suggest some weaknesses?
    - What areas do I want to grow in as a leader?

- As you continue your pursuit of great leadership, you will find this tool so helpful that over the years you will end up filling several journal notebooks. To make it easier to retrieve your thoughts, we have provided the "Easy-Recap Index" on the last pages at the back. Once you have completed this volume, go back over your entries (you can use the brief titles you created on the left-hand pages), and enter the entry titles into this index. Later, when you want to find something you wrote in the past, it will be easy to find it.

- At certain points—once a month, once a quarter, or at least every six months—set some time aside to go back over your entries and reflect on what you have written. What key themes do you see? What common threads weave their way through your entries? What key principles are you uncovering? Begin a list. You can use the pages opposite the Easy-Recap Index pages; they are designed to capture these thoughts.

- The purpose of this journal is to help you in your growth as a leader. As you begin to reflect more deliberately and more systematically on your leadership (which you will with this journal), you will begin to see how much material is out there on leadership (if you haven't already!). To help you figure out what you need from this often bewildering array of resources, we have created a framework that makes sense of all these offerings. We recommend you read *Great Leadership: What It Is and What It Takes in a Complex World* or *The Clock Tower*, both by Antony Bell. They provide you with a framework that will help you identify the resources most relevant to the challenges you face and the direction you want to go in.

This page is intentionally left blank. Use it to write a quick subject title opposite each entry, which will help you when you come to complete the Easy-Recap Index at the back. You can also use this page to make additional comments when you come back and look over your notes.

Great leadership is a matter of both character and competence.
You need both. Just like the two wings of an aircraft,
you can't have one without the other.

This page is intentionally left blank. Use it to write a quick subject title opposite each entry, which will help you when you come to complete the Easy-Recap Index at the back. You can also use this page to make additional comments when you come back and look over your notes.

*Character in leadership is about
pursuing noble ends with noble means.*

This page is intentionally left blank. Use it to write a quick subject title opposite each entry, which will help you when you come to complete the Easy-Recap Index at the back. You can also use this page to make additional comments when you come back and look over your notes.

Competence in leadership is applying knowledge, skill, and talent to those noble ends and noble means.

This page is intentionally left blank. Use it to write a quick subject title opposite each entry, which will help you when you come to complete the Easy-Recap Index at the back. You can also use this page to make additional comments when you come back and look over your notes.

Competence can get you to the table. Character will keep you there.

This page is intentionally left blank. Use it to write a quick subject title opposite each entry, which will help you when you come to complete the Easy-Recap Index at the back. You can also use this page to make additional comments when you come back and look over your notes.

> Great leaders ask questions—to listen better, to provoke thinking, to stimulate learning . . . and sometimes to get answers.

This page is intentionally left blank. Use it to write a quick subject title opposite each entry, which will help you when you come to complete the Easy-Recap Index at the back. You can also use this page to make additional comments when you come back and look over your notes.

Don't be concerned about style, spelling or grammar. This journal is for your own eyes and for your own private consumption. You're not writing to impress . . . you are writing to think.

This page is intentionally left blank. Use it to write a quick subject title opposite each entry, which will help you when you come to complete the Easy-Recap Index at the back. You can also use this page to make additional comments when you come back and look over your notes.

Great leaders ask questions. Your journal is a great place to reflect on questions . . . and to note the questions you want to ask others.

This page is intentionally left blank. Use it to write a quick subject title opposite each entry, which will help you when you come to complete the Easy-Recap Index at the back. You can also use this page to make additional comments when you come back and look over your notes.

"Great and good are seldom the same man," Churchill once observed. In other words, competence and character are a rare combination. Pursuing both is pursuing greatness.

This page is intentionally left blank. Use it to write a quick subject title opposite each entry, which will help you when you come to complete the Easy-Recap Index at the back. You can also use this page to make additional comments when you come back and look over your notes.

Chinese bamboo trees lie dormant for four to five years, and then in a six-week period, they grow 90 feet. Question: Do they take six weeks to grow, or five years and six weeks?

This page is intentionally left blank. Use it to write a quick subject title opposite each entry, which will help you when you come to complete the Easy-Recap Index at the back. You can also use this page to make additional comments when you come back and look over your notes.

The answer: Five years and six weeks! They need to be watered and nurtured all through the five years. Leadership growth is like that: keep watering, and the growth will come, sometimes dramatically.

This page is intentionally left blank. Use it to write a quick subject title opposite each entry, which will help you when you come to complete the Easy-Recap Index at the back. You can also use this page to make additional comments when you come back and look over your notes.

Great leaders are patient and persistent about their own development. They understand that it takes time.

This page is intentionally left blank. Use it to write a quick subject title opposite each entry, which will help you when you come to complete the Easy-Recap Index at the back. You can also use this page to make additional comments when you come back and look over your notes.

> *Great leaders are readers, because at heart, great leaders are learners. And reading is a great learning tool. Use your journal to reflect on what you are reading.*

This page is intentionally left blank. Use it to write a quick subject title opposite each entry, which will help you when you come to complete the Easy-Recap Index at the back. You can also use this page to make additional comments when you come back and look over your notes.

"I will study and prepare," Abraham Lincoln once said, *"and perhaps my day will come."* He was a constant learner; even when his day eventually came, he still kept learning.

This page is intentionally left blank. Use it to write a quick subject title opposite each entry, which will help you when you come to complete the Easy-Recap Index at the back. You can also use this page to make additional comments when you come back and look over your notes.

What leadership lessons do you observe from the movies you've seen or the TV shows you watch? Reflect on them in your journal.

This page is intentionally left blank. Use it to write a quick subject title opposite each entry, which will help you when you come to complete the Easy-Recap Index at the back. You can also use this page to make additional comments when you come back and look over your notes.

> Humor not only relieves tension; it also strengthens people's capacity to embrace yet more tension. What humor can you record in your journal that you can use with the people you lead?

This page is intentionally left blank. Use it to write a quick subject title opposite each entry, which will help you when you come to complete the Easy-Recap Index at the back. You can also use this page to make additional comments when you come back and look over your notes.

The pen has been called a mental crowbar, and rightly so: it pries out thoughts embedded beneath the surface of our subconscious, and exposes them to our scrutiny so that we can mold, massage, shape . . . and deliver them.

This page is intentionally left blank. Use it to write a quick subject title opposite each entry, which will help you when you come to complete the Easy-Recap Index at the back. You can also use this page to make additional comments when you come back and look over your notes.

> *At the heart of leadership is the leader's worldview—how we look at life, its meaning, its purpose, the nature of mankind, the existence and nature of God. Much of it is unconscious, but it still defines our leadership.*

This page is intentionally left blank. Use it to write a quick subject title opposite each entry, which will help you when you come to complete the Easy-Recap Index at the back. You can also use this page to make additional comments when you come back and look over your notes.

As you explore great leadership, you will inevitably reflect on your worldview. Let these pages help you in your reflection, and if the answers aren't there, note the questions. It's indispensable to great leadership.

This page is intentionally left blank. Use it to write a quick subject title opposite each entry, which will help you when you come to complete the Easy-Recap Index at the back. You can also use this page to make additional comments when you come back and look over your notes.

> The path to great leadership is above all an internal path. At least, that's where it starts. Without the journey inside, there can be no greatness outside. This journal is a logbook for the journey inside.

This page is intentionally left blank. Use it to write a quick subject title opposite each entry, which will help you when you come to complete the Easy-Recap Index at the back. You can also use this page to make additional comments when you come back and look over your notes.

> "Courage," Churchill observed, "is what it takes to stand up and speak; courage is also what it takes to sit down and listen." What kind of courage do you currently need in your leadership role?

This page is intentionally left blank. Use it to write a quick subject title opposite each entry, which will help you when you come to complete the Easy-Recap Index at the back. You can also use this page to make additional comments when you come back and look over your notes.

What are some of the deep values you hold that are beginning to surface through these pages?
Great leaders lead by values more than by charisma.

This page is intentionally left blank. Use it to write a quick subject title opposite each entry, which will help you when you come to complete the Easy-Recap Index at the back. You can also use this page to make additional comments when you come back and look over your notes.

"O would some power the gift to give us to see ourselves as others see us! It would from many a blunder free us." (Robert Burns). Consider your Leadership Journal as a tool for self-awareness.

This page is intentionally left blank. Use it to write a quick subject title opposite each entry, which will help you when you come to complete the Easy-Recap Index at the back. You can also use this page to make additional comments when you come back and look over your notes.

> *Is this a tough time in your leadership? If it is,
> or when such a time comes, keep learning, and don't retreat.
> As Churchill put it, "If you're going through hell, keep going."*

This page is intentionally left blank. Use it to write a quick subject title opposite each entry, which will help you when you come to complete the Easy-Recap Index at the back. You can also use this page to make additional comments when you come back and look over your notes.

Great leaders are story makers. The people they lead play critical roles as the story unfolds, and when new people come on, great leaders write them into a vital role in the story line. Use these pages to reflect on the story you are crafting.

This page is intentionally left blank. Use it to write a quick subject title opposite each entry, which will help you when you come to complete the Easy-Recap Index at the back. You can also use this page to make additional comments when you come back and look over your notes.

> Great leaders are students: students of themselves, students of the people they lead, and students of great leadership.

This page is intentionally left blank. Use it to write a quick subject title opposite each entry, which will help you when you come to complete the Easy-Recap Index at the back. You can also use this page to make additional comments when you come back and look over your notes.

"Leadership and learning are indispensable to each other."
The words of President John F. Kennedy,
an avid reader and a committed learner.

This page is intentionally left blank. Use it to write a quick subject title opposite each entry, which will help you when you come to complete the Easy-Recap Index at the back. You can also use this page to make additional comments when you come back and look over your notes.

*Distance is the enemy of impact.
You cannot deeply impact someone without getting close to them.
Direct involvement is indispensable.*

This page is intentionally left blank. Use it to write a quick subject title opposite each entry, which will help you when you come to complete the Easy-Recap Index at the back. You can also use this page to make additional comments when you come back and look over your notes.

Observe the people you lead: what strengths do you see? What could you do to help them strengthen those strengths? Jot down some thoughts in this journal.

This page is intentionally left blank. Use it to write a quick subject title opposite each entry, which will help you when you come to complete the Easy-Recap Index at the back. You can also use this page to make additional comments when you come back and look over your notes.

Observe the people you lead: is there anything you see that could potentially derail them? Is it time for a courageous conversation?

This page is intentionally left blank. Use it to write a quick subject title opposite each entry, which will help you when you come to complete the Easy-Recap Index at the back. You can also use this page to make additional comments when you come back and look over your notes.

> Writing is the midwife of creative thought. The very act of writing produces ideas that wouldn't exist without picking up a pen. Great leaders write—to help them think.

This page is intentionally left blank. Use it to write a quick subject title opposite each entry, which will help you when you come to complete the Easy-Recap Index at the back. You can also use this page to make additional comments when you come back and look over your notes.

In your current role are there people who don't report to you directly, but whom you could help in their own growth?

This page is intentionally left blank. Use it to write a quick subject title opposite each entry, which will help you when you come to complete the Easy-Recap Index at the back. You can also use this page to make additional comments when you come back and look over your notes.

The most significant thing about an organization is what goes on in the minds of its leaders. Think about what you think, because what you think will shape what you do.

This page is intentionally left blank. Use it to write a quick subject title opposite each entry, which will help you when you come to complete the Easy-Recap Index at the back. You can also use this page to make additional comments when you come back and look over your notes.

> *To be a student of great leadership, you need a framework—one that pulls together all the different elements of leadership into a coherent whole.*

This page is intentionally left blank. Use it to write a quick subject title opposite each entry, which will help you when you come to complete the Easy-Recap Index at the back. You can also use this page to make additional comments when you come back and look over your notes.

[Perspective is the ability to see an object miles away
in relationship to an object right before us.
Perspective is essential to great leadership.]

This page is intentionally left blank. Use it to write a quick subject title opposite each entry, which will help you when you come to complete the Easy-Recap Index at the back. You can also use this page to make additional comments when you come back and look over your notes.

Perspective allows us to place the present—what is before us—in the context of the future—what lies ahead of us.

This page is intentionally left blank. Use it to write a quick subject title opposite each entry, which will help you when you come to complete the Easy-Recap Index at the back. You can also use this page to make additional comments when you come back and look over your notes.

*Don't be afraid to record your failures on these pages.
All leaders fail. Great leaders reflect on their failures.*

This page is intentionally left blank. Use it to write a quick subject title opposite each entry, which will help you when you come to complete the Easy-Recap Index at the back. You can also use this page to make additional comments when you come back and look over your notes.

> Great leaders are teachers. They not only understand and exercise great leadership, they also pass it on. This may be the greatest differentiator between good leaders and great leaders: great leaders teach others to become great leaders.

This page is intentionally left blank. Use it to write a quick subject title opposite each entry, which will help you when you come to complete the Easy-Recap Index at the back. You can also use this page to make additional comments when you come back and look over your notes.

> Great leaders think creatively about their communications. Their first instinct is not an email. They look for different, even unusual ways to convey a message in a way it will be remembered.

This page is intentionally left blank. Use it to write a quick subject title opposite each entry, which will help you when you come to complete the Easy-Recap Index at the back. You can also use this page to make additional comments when you come back and look over your notes.

*Learning never stops. As John Wooden put it,
"It's what you learn after you know it all that counts."*

This page is intentionally left blank. Use it to write a quick subject title opposite each entry, which will help you when you come to complete the Easy-Recap Index at the back. You can also use this page to make additional comments when you come back and look over your notes.

Movies about teachers tell us much about great leadership. Watch (or watch again) movies like The Emperor's Club, Freedom Writers, Lean on Me, *and* Remember the Titans. *What do you discover about great leadership?*

This page is intentionally left blank. Use it to write a quick subject title opposite each entry, which will help you when you come to complete the Easy-Recap Index at the back. You can also use this page to make additional comments when you come back and look over your notes.

At some point, each one of us is required to act with courage. As Martin Luther King Jr. put it, "The ultimate measure of a man is not where he stands in moments of comfort and convenience, but where he stands at times of challenge and controversy."

This page is intentionally left blank. Use it to write a quick subject title opposite each entry, which will help you when you come to complete the Easy-Recap Index at the back. You can also use this page to make additional comments when you come back and look over your notes.

> As a leader, you are inevitably an example. Pope Gregory the Great put it this way: "He who is required by the necessity of his position to speak the highest things is compelled by the same necessity to exemplify the highest things."

This page is intentionally left blank. Use it to write a quick subject title opposite each entry, which will help you when you come to complete the Easy-Recap Index at the back. You can also use this page to make additional comments when you come back and look over your notes.

Samuel Johnson once stated that "Integrity without knowledge is weak and useless, and knowledge without integrity is dangerous and dreadful." That's a potent statement for the necessity of both character ("integrity") and competence ("knowledge").

From the Easy-Recap Index, do you see some key themes? Some common threads? Some key principles? Jot them down below.

Easy-Recap Index

Page	Date	Subject

From the Easy-Recap Index, do you see some key themes? Some common threads? Some key principles? Jot them down below.

Easy-Recap Index

Page	Date	Subject

From the Easy-Recap Index, do you see some key themes? Some common threads? Some key principles? Jot them down below.

Easy-Recap Index

Page	Date	Subject

From the Easy-Recap Index, do you see some key themes? Some common threads? Some key principles? Jot them down below.

Easy-Recap Index

Page	Date	Subject

*For more resources from LeaderDevelopment Inc.,
visit our website at www.leaderdevelopmentinc.com.*

www.ingramcontent.com/pod-product-compliance
Lightning Source LLC
Chambersburg PA
CBHW030524100426
42813CB00001B/142